STRAY

Allison LaSorda

icehouse poetry
an imprint of Goose Lane Editions

Edited by Linda Besner.
Cover and page design by Julie Scriver.
Cover image copyright © 2008 "Feather" by Andrew Maruska, AndrewMaruska.com.
Printed in Canada.
10 9 8 7 6 5 4 3 2 1
Printed in Canada.

Library and Archives Canada Cataloguing in Publication

LaSorda, Allison, author
    Stray / Allison LaSorda.

Poems.
Issued in print and electronic formats.
ISBN 978-0-86492-978-5 (paperback).--ISBN 978-0-86492-979-2 (epub).--
ISBN 978-0-86492-980-8 (mobi)

    I. Title.

PS8623.A7756S77 2017   C811'.6   C2016-907045-X
                                           C2016-907046-8

We acknowledge the generous support of the Government of Canada, the Canada Council for the Arts, and the Government of New Brunswick.

Goose Lane Editions
500 Beaverbrook Court, Suite 330
Fredericton, New Brunswick
CANADA E3B 5X4
www.gooselane.com

STRAY

Contents

MEAT

FISH

Backstroke

I was on the other line
when you were dying, Daddio.
Off-duty, smoothing things over
with a guy whose face
was a pot-holed wharf.

He promised me glory.
I became a decorated lifeguard.

You went dim, seasick
in some holy buoyancy,
counting an eel's inner rings
to predict the tides.

Tomorrow, a lineup of hours
calling my bluff.
I left him, Pops,
'cause you hated to see me cry.
I hid a nerve in visions:

mermaid purses and tongue stones
washed to shore. Spectacular coughs
barking from marine mammoths.

Guilt shifted its gills,
a known bottom-feeder.
While I was picnicking
by the coast,
you called to tell me
I walked with confidence.

Hit the Beach

Teenagers have cornered the market
on attention from the elders.
This might be my last chance.

I can fight the aging process.
Watch me become another person,
just bring me one more drink.

My softness is absorbent. Pray,
set me free in malleability, or else
accept the burden of clean-up duty.

A shifting silhouette is ripe for typecasting.
My flesh wobbles as I trample
a castle's remains, betrayed by high tide.

I bask in the disdain. Am I different yet?
Had I muscle tone or an observable waist,
I'd be trusted to deliver my own meaning.

If my temperament
is more sand trap than sandbar,
how can I ever grow up?

The Smallest Island

i.

You hold your breath
so long the swimming teacher
plucks you from the shallows.

An empty parking lot
fumes in your belly.

A reverse splash — gasp,
your grin flipped onto the tiles.
The first dessert you ever tasted
whips itself into reflux.

As if all the trees in the world
were housed,
there are no imaginations left.

ii.

Beach-bound. You launch
out, toes spread, boogie board
jouncing into whitecaps.

The waves float plastic
as you paddle
and you're swallowed
in sea glass and cans,

undertow crashing knee
to coral. Blood drifts
like jellyfish
across your goggles.

iii.

You dig a fingernail
into turquoise vinyl.

Your sister turns over
in a lawn chair, her skin
glossy and marked by the straps.

While handstanding, you see
her sandal drift to the deep end.
It settles amid ant clusters
at pool bottom.
You dive to rescue it,
but she throws it back. *Fetch.*

iv.

You laugh until the
corners of your mouth
crack. The tide
approaches steadily.

Summers blur into
one sloppy memory —
Disney is Wasaga is Cape Cod.

Photos from this day
are sun-bleached. You,
hand-on-hip on the boardwalk.
Your sister, stained
with two melted scoops;

a relative you don't recognize
follows her, carrying plastic buckets.
What's inside them?

Mother buries you
on the beach until only
your face feels air.

Palm trees cut triangles
of shadow onto the water.

Dog Star

The aquarium in the bar needs cleaning.
A lion fish paddles listlessly
towards patrons' cartoon imaginations.

Christmas lights draped across the glass
bring us closer to the experience of stars
than real stars. We witness the precise moment
twinkle stars burn out and so, if a child asks,
we can explain why they vanish into dark.

Inside me a hare skitters.
A man installed it as my spirit animal,
but it doesn't fit right. I hate running. I prefer dogs.

I've seen dog jealousy and the human need
to point it out, shame the sentiment away.

Who could say I'm a traitor as my tongue
lolls out, as I tell each person I've befriended:
I'm sorry for your loss, there's always next year.

Playdate

You've got me where you want me
but what wants remain are paltry;
I've bailed, searching out the lick
in the split crow footprint of your spit,
left to dry white astride my thighs.
Let me rinse this off and spy
what crops up in the flailing bouts
of each time you couldn't come out.
Playing with you is like teaching
a humpback whale how not to breach.

The Sea Is All about Us

Am I worried about it? Yes
and no and no and yes,
in no particular order.

Here's where it comes in,
the sense that it's always leaving.
Today it's unswimmable.

I stand at Big Sur's lip,
unbound by a sense of
plummeting I've shared
in peaks with their own charm.
Water froths like milk.

The temperature is climbing,
and I can't understand
what a conveyor belt
has to do with undertow.

It could mean I've homed in
on shame's root. My anxiety's
origin story isn't in bleached reefs
or fault lines, it's in maws
gaping with *somedays*.

Waves dash between rocks
until they're foamy as saliva
bubbled through teeth.

I breathe a furrow into my forehead
and carry this towel like a shield.

Shark Year

When I died the first time,
I got a sinking feeling.

It's easier to think *I can't*
than *I don't want to.*

With an imposed trajectory,
a valiant obstacle in my course,
I'm off the hook.

Leisure is to labour
as is compromise to fervour.

The second time,
I want to be flesh
chummed by bleachers
of serrated teeth.

Rolled up in a carpet
and plunked into the sea.

No One Knows I'm Gone

In the thick of it you'd brighten
at the sight of me, tracing
the sternum bulge beneath my skin.

My insides were the empty hull
of a lode ship for an unnamed
pilot, a conveyance withstanding
heavy seas. Memory trick:
frayed whitecaps prompt waiting.

As my body dried out,
I looked for a swimmer —
the waking wet, sleeping wide,
a blonde who wouldn't Russify.

Because I lied about everything
except my height, gravesite
and Walkyr bloodlines,
there was no safety
between our legs.

Youthless

Backswimmers skitter on stagnant water,
gurgle-mouthed as the pond dips.

My real morning face
hosts bereavement in a flush
that doesn't stay.

No wind. The vessel mired.
An egg carton is a cardboard cradle.

I neglect each question I've raised.
Abandon these orphans

in the stink of algal wonder,
beady eyes wondering why.
Cut to the warm part. My pollywogs

grow legs, hop into backyard pool filters
and only need me
to resent where they came from.

Elver

Hook an eel and reel it in. It wraps around my hand
and constricts like a boa. My cousin yells to hurry,
get the lure out — but the muscle, the persistence grips.

For the past week I've been visiting. I hug people,
see them pause to sculpt an answer.
Someone concedes they last saw me at a funeral.

Blueberries wither in an old ice cream bucket.
Things grow faster than I remember; I eat quickly.

Clouds look different, more cheerful.
Ancestors made nuisances of themselves here, casting
their nets, planting, skills that have long left my blood.

A high school friend tours me around the valley sites:
the pig farm he can't afford will be developed;
this used to be *that*. The drive makes me ravenous.

Stay in his childhood bedroom. He tells me he used to open
a drawer to lock himself in when he got in trouble.
I open the drawer while I undress.

Fish & Bird

The smallest cut has the fewest needs.
The largest cut's requirements surpass
our abilities. That slit's impossible to find
unless by chance, and then proves tough
to classify. Recognizable as flesh, not slash
or butterfly, lance or scrape; neither prepared
event nor accident. It exists between, a split
virtually in twain. The largest cut plumbs
unreachable depths, swims with blind,
frightening fish. Its unlimited closets,
hidden attics, shake with captured wind
from the hubbub of birds' wings.
To call it a sinkhole mightn't be wrong.
The smallest cut is childhood, every memory
a splinter. The largest cut is your potential,
beckoning with inborn chirps like everything
you couldn't say, and everything you did.

BIRD

The First One's Always Free

If you were still mine,
my sweet Jubilee, I'd bother
to come up with sap to spew.

I can't name a specific thing
I'd do for you, but maybe
knowing is better than doing.

Who in their right mind
doesn't want to be defined
by each person they've left?

Jubilee, remember our meet-cute?
Can you see beyond prophecy
and follow the interstate away

from a house of ill repute?
I can't, so tell me to cool it
or refill me with the *oh you*s

you do so well, uncultured
ten-month pearls, words
clip-on gold for want of praise.

Sweet, when you left I broke down
from the upside, lurching past
the space within a barren cleft.

If we'd rather deal in dialects
or muck around in sludge
we sling to share, why bother?

Out of the Chorus

My barynya is just extraordinary.
I beat my body like a drum. Sarafans
swirl until vermilion embroidery blurs
to great frenetic effect for a wannabe tsar.

I would rather have been a ballerina,
but I inherited the folksy costume.
The audience gathers theatre side.
Years of sad salt buildup
crusted around my eyes, fusing
with gold leaf for an alarming mask.

I was born in the eyelashes of a hurricane:
it rained dog pelts, relieving my mother
from the sounds of pulsing monitors.
She knew my dancer's destiny.
I'd squatted and leapt in utero, charting
the records broken in every test.

We out-Cossack the Cossacks, my partners say.
Arm-flapping, toe-tapping Lezgi eagles and swans,
hordes of one-trick ponies — we're disciples
of attention, raised and kept solely to perform.
I can't speak. My body spells out *lockup* for me.

Weather

The weather vane on the coop behind our house
always points south. The joint is rusted.
No forecasts worthy to report.

Our school bus circles the forest that persists
on the escarpment. Kids point, foreheads smearing
windows, and say, *That's where the dead girl was found.*
Then trade snacks. The dump site
a landmark, like where one of us used to live.

Count the drainage pipes,
think on the tug of ditch.
When it rains, it rains.

A kid says willows are the saddest trees,
but they're rare. You picture cattails
pocking a resting place, uneasy birds
that mistake her hair for brome.

Sultry air a yoke around the neck.
Nothing moves.
Pull away, and it tightens.

The forest is not for us, though we talk trees
till we stop remembering. Ginkgos, if female,
drop putrid seeds come autumn. Their scent
on the ground, on the wind, while days get shorter.

Deer Stand

You place yourself into a photo
of a hunting blind on stilts
above tall grass, the area blasted
with pre-sunset light.
You do not think beyond the shot.
The clearing in the forest
is your projection, elastic and foolish.
For hours you stare at the image
to solve a magic eye painting:
the composition of a hurricane
brews behind the silver birch,
its force dispelling focus
from the deer stand. You're the buck,
ambling without dread at the foot
of a ladder. Your body, an eight-point
slingshot, tensed for a divine moment
that must be seized and mounted, or else
forgotten. A display of love, you cut
cool air with your trace, not thinking
about suddenly disappearing.

Reply to the Shepherd

Without expecting gentleness,
I take my moral code in stride.

Flash to stark undress. The herder
uses a strong-eye and heel approach.

In truth, I yield easily. It's mind-blowing,
how fast he rubs off on me.

Men beg to fumble change
deep in my pocket, to shoot blanks
against an open, empty locket.

I'll only get drunk enough
to achieve a higher pastoral plane,

rapt, dropping clothes with a hypnotic clap
every time someone says *leave*.

Fluid Dynamics

I'm only awake to his body
while asleep at the wheel,
spinning into traffic cams
I didn't see until the last moment.

That's not true — watching myself
being watched is a new ball game,
the kind with chandeliers.

I want to unsee all the passed-out
cocktail hours of my life, glowering
in the glow of hunting décor.

Listen, I would never Jolene your man,
but he may not put up a fight.
He's solid when everything's sopping,
a barrel-aged object of objection.

One time, his double swayed me
south of where I'm supposed to be:
stirred into a mind's eye levity.
I want a love that flows preternaturally.

Midsummer Signal

O, it was sunny above the cloudline.
I climbed steep ridges,
suffered shrub-bloodied ankles
to call you and left the same
message each time.
Once, armed to the nines
with appraisals, guts spun
inside me like soft serve.
I described the archipelago
until your mailbox was full.
Rinsed my wounds
in brackish water.
In a crumbling castle,
I traversed a velvet rope
to the royal weapon room
and counted so many guns
I got vertigo.
On a guided tour, I learned
that when the sun shines
for years on leather wallpaper,
it splits and shrivels; storied lore
in colours is ruined slowly
over time, as everything is.
Lo, sometimes even in the lap
of baroque luxury,
you can't escape daylight.

The Wetlands Draw Conclusions

Three people saw me naked with Mercury in retrograde.
Each a Sagittarius, they had nothing in common.
The sky fell in blurry chunks at my side.

My Leo died, is why. His particular sneeze, his urges,
noted then thrown out on a crumpled sheet.
You can't unsee the crease in paper once you fold it.

In my binoculars' beam, a grackle sunned itself
upon the atmospheric rubble, puzzled, but content
to shine. There may not be light enough for all of us.

Living is waving your arms for help in pitch dark.
The fire-signs took me to a swamp with live, rowdy things:
flowering water, grass electric with hum, ribbit, tweet.

I cleaved the wetlands to chase them back to city grid.
A new orbit started. As though it couldn't wait.
If they had a birding goal, I didn't find their blue jay.

Party Favours

Dressed as Maximilian Kolbe on All Saints' Day
but you found no glory. You looked good in stripes.
By Christmas you stopped gleaming in the light.
You put a puss on, insistent, carving out your place.
Aside from sex-sputtering nightmares you're warped inside.
Party favours are handcuffs; cake is dead weight.
Unwrap the companion gift of permanent high tide.

Glory Days

I quit music for Lent, but sighed
so loud a tune came out.

See, I can never tell
how I want things to be.
That's why I'm unlovable
or at least hard to please.

I want every song sung by Springsteen.
I need a boss for my home life.

Sketch me the monuments
I tried to forget. Let's meet halfway
in a green card marriage, so I can swaddle
my bouncing baby boys to *Born in the U.S.A.*

I figure Bruce dreams the same
way he sings, plainly, earnestness
drawn out so clear I am embarrassed
by my secrecy, by all his feelings,
eyes closed for the good parts.
There's a dream there
and I've earned my slice.

Lime Kiln Ruins

Your wolf birds are starting to show.
I pretend not to notice.
On this trail winds are shushing,
crows croaking over dead
grass tracts. Clustered ferns dither
and bounce, we practise leaf peeping.

Those kids know the route better
and shimmy up the rock face
where we skidded with their dog Sierra.
I'm tired of this struggle to stay
upright on slick ground, of overhearing
and being afraid to heed. In a day

you'll be gone east, tucked in
or haunting the river beasts
of another bed, but not too deeply;
I'll be central, sleeping,
splashing around. We've lived
in all the same places, settled

bodies in ditches, buried fools.
Sierra barks somewhere uphill.
Your stiffened posture mimics
the cliff. Where are all the human,
earthly things?

My passerines become visible.
You're scattering seeds.
We share this swift trail, the mist
rising off the escarpment,
each red tree fatigued and huffing.

The End of Grief

When the end of grief was announced
the houses on our street
slouched until all were lopsided.
Those of us who dwell
on the mysteries of our dead
wedge our bodies into the foundations.
We want as long as possible to figure out
what might be beautiful about loss.
The river rushes anew,
water so opaque it looks
pleated. We want clothing
that hangs as loose as river.
Knock on the underside
of floors but nobody answers —
this, too, is a sign. The houses
heave with our pulses.
Children whisper through dirt
that since the declaration
and resultant slanting of their beds,
they only dream of flying.
We feel sorry for them.
Our dreams do chores.
They self-repair, dig trenches,
throw leaves into gutters clogged
with competing impulses:
eke out consolation
in what's fixed, or hazard
the pang of stranger gravity.

Fraterville Coal Mine

We are all praying for air to support us,
but it is getting so bad without any air.

In the absence of air
did it feel like your body split
or tempered?

Ellen, I want you to live right
and come to heaven.

There are things
you should know, Jacob.
I live according to my impulses
part time. Other men paw
the sticky ladder of my neck bones
as they stoop over me too fast,
too close to the woodstove.

Raise the children the best you can.
Goodbye Ellen, goodbye Lily,
goodbye Jemmie, goodbye Horace.

I woke the children
as you puttered into the mine.
Lily's mute since the nightmares,
Jemmie's a real middle child,
Horace has something to live up to.
Elbert is filled with your blood,
I am filled with Eddie's.
Each kid slipped
too quick from my frame,
breathed up all the wind.

Oh, how I wish to be with you, goodbye.

I let the horses out that night
to buy some time in bed.
I have a favourite child.
Your face will be indelible,
your nakedness will fade.
I'm afraid that nothing
is fast approaching.

We are together.

What did it look like within the roof fall?
An expected hush, wet cotton?
Or colours I can't thread together,
a caterwauling stirring dust
until the impulse stopped.

Is 25 minutes after two.
There is a few of us alive yet.

I cave in. Time becomes nature.
You spill through the mouth
of a mountain.

Perseids

You shave paint from shingles for days
in a way so angry it's graceful.
Yellow confetti blankets the ground.
Our archives are returning to you,
not in paint, not even in colours,
but in repetitive tasks.
Today, my work is to transcribe.
I write *clumsy*, then cross it out.
The list could become a map,
and if you follow it, you might fall.
Instead I jot *accomplished*, alongside
other words you've long disowned,
and in their foreignness I hope
to confer some illumination.
The future is sealed
because night will come.
In sleep we walk through unlocked doors
to planets with perfect, humid air.
Your body is exhausted, crouched
and tender even in recovery.
As we trade pillows,
Perseid meteors dash across the night.
Come morning, you're launched
onto scaffolding.
That feeling, like watching someone
use your furniture as if it were theirs.

Ricochet

A body walks by
on my legs.
Stretched out, I
recollect, watch
myself become
a child, immobile,
in a place
that captures
youth and holds
it hostage. Supple
limbs propel
and flex, then fade,
ache and stiffen.
Age implying loss
of movement:
to be desiccated
into shape.
There's a point
at which one
cannot reconsider.
It's the same place
where I realize
I've never
been weightless.
In fact, I'm sinking
into quiet.
Where to go
if one is eager
to forge ahead?
Towards the sound
of the rightful
owner.

In a twitch of tendons
I clutch elastic
sole skin, girlish
before it got bullied
by plough-trenches
and barrenness.
A trail wears out
from door to
field to grassy
cellar to roadside
stand and back.
No mistakes.
Always a return
route tracing
the boomerang
path of thoughts.
My knees buckle.

Coven

Till I was sixteen, I thought Sylvia Plath
put her head in a lit oven.

I've never wanted anything
enough to melt my face off.

In the evening, I pick my stigmata
scabs, and show myself out.

I slap my face three times
and come like Beetlejuice.

It's the *why not* that stings.
How stubborn I'd prefer to be.

My beard of bees mourns
razor burn in a sallow sink.

I've not wanted plenty, a dead dad,
arts asking too much from their faker.

MEAT

More or Less at the Canal

Something about the criss-cross of the contrails today made me
nauseated. I read about a father-son murder-suicide one town over.
I conjured a teenager into a pattern of the part he'd play. But the
boy was only six. It has to do with dimension: a spider, magnified
in a grotesque shadow, racing across my ceiling. I'll have to kill it.
I can't live my remaining years with the responsibility for crushing
insects. It's about proving something. You'd admire the way I kept
rolling on my bike from the lift-lock into the dark. I heard the glass
and felt the shards around my legs like rain. I hyperventilated to
keep the tires full. Because you once told me sleeping was one of
the things I ruined for you, that holding me was like a hailstorm,
and I believed it all.

Horses

Say *horses* and my hands fill with hay,
I'm at the fences hoping for affection.
Skipping ropes were reins
to control each other in the baseball diamond.
Turns taken as jockey or racer,
girls asserting themselves as Appaloosas,
or subduing their wildness to be corralled.
Blank pages quickly filled with horses
drawn when I wasn't riding horses.
Pastern, snip, socks, blazes and stars,
and the origins of their expression.
Say *rodeo* and I can't associate.
In the saloon last night was a Stetson
on a man other men lined up to talk to.
I heard a cowboy say the mechanical bull
grip is different from the one for riding broncos,
but the how was swallowed by the crowd.
I'm not obliged to stay here
and watch history hammer nails into itself.
My future is about to break an ankle.
I thought of this in the ladies' room
where in eyeliner a mirror asked,
what are you looking at.

Race, Stock, Kin

To scout the scavengers,
coax them across the median
with fast food bait. A grand passage,
like hay worked through a bowel.

The quills and fur of the departed
remain alight with hibernation's glow.
I catalogue roadkill by the overpass,
measure their wounds against
the circumference of to-go cup lids.

Once dead we all disappoint someone.
On the highway's gravel shoulder,
life dribbles out of bottlenecks
like a slo-mo New Year's Eve.

I ration time in pepperettes
and diesel prices. Find me amidst
trophies, defending a pedigree.

Home Team

I apologize for connective instincts,
like how I think of my father
each time I eat a nectarine.

I am the grandbaby of a MLB player.
Yes, two generations away from talent.
I wear my goals and failures like ankle weights.
Take me out. I could learn to make him proud.

Years pile up enough to swagger.
It's on me to hew time into palatable chunks.
I think of my children with each bicep curl.

My body is a joke —
maybe you've heard it before?
It lives in an overpriced apartment,
prefigures its own dysmorphia.

I started out too far behind, that is,
was born late in the day. Warmth
pours into me. I can't retain it.
Sun slides off my back. The burn
is aimless, so I carry, carry, carry.

Natural Crime

I allow myself skin, not the meat of the animal.
It's better to eat what will grow back.
This I learned from a children's program
that turned out to be sponsored by endemic plants.

Look at the blazing sun refracting
a magenta shroud for city buildings.
Nature was once America's
pastime, but times are tough.

The matryoshka doll in an orca's belly
bleeps its location to marine biologists.
Whales are the new heartthrobs, one day
they'll fulfill their purpose, then disappear.

I plated the whole fish with its lidless eye,
reflecting that I'd never scaled, seldom gutted.
Evolution gives me hope that my children will be
immune to mosquitoes, which might mean they'll be tasteless.

Have you ever heard of the funnel theory?
Bred for size, we'll shrink to occupy Victorian dollhouses.
Ultimately, we'll succumb to the influence of ant colonies
who'll chant: *Behold the twilight of your species.*

Regard the blood moon while a man howls.
An untraceable myth has failed us.

Summer Vacation

This is not my first memory,
but the first I care to talk about.
It's summer. I weep, silent,
as doctors test my reflexes.
My friends ride bikes
without training wheels.
At night I count cricket chirps.
By an open window I pick skin
raw as it itches with insomnia.
The dentist retrofits me
with canines that curve, sharp,
adept at crushing bone.
Days flop their uniform bodies.
I learn a new means of chewing.
Carrion tastes of all the charred flesh
I've molared on backyard patios;
it reminds me of meaningful
eye contact shared with raccoons
and dogs, as if to say,
we are all hungry.
If you're just joining me,
blood has stained my chin,
replacing my puberty's
alabaster glow. I yearn
for a domain that spreads
like a spangled oil slick.
My family lets me loose.

Messages from Thunder Bay

Tonight will be my first night in my new tent. I'm looking forward to a view of morning from the inside.

We accidentally sent a smoke signal to the nearby camp.

Sorry about the telephone last night. It was fine for a while but then cut out. You have a wonderful voice. I've always told you.

People keep asking me about the outside — outside being home. I have a low tolerance for nostalgia and ghost stories, so I fashion a tinder nest as words unravel their loops.

I find kismet in stomped out campfires and blue tarps luffing dust out of the ground.

We press skipping stones to sleeping feet in hopes the double dutch rope will rock our dreams.

I think I'm starting to look like a clear-cut.

I'm miserable. Haven't had time to take a nap. I know you're probably not expecting much, but if you're expecting anything at all you might be expecting too much.

Down with Exhaustion

Dank sunrise below Pink Mountain.
You groan out of your tent,
stretching the heels of your hands
onto the pad of beige gravel.

In the bush you find vertebrae in owl pellets
and rickety moose calves learning
to pull choice branches with their lips.

All you can think is, I'd kill
for some furniture, a carpet,
an uncomfortable desk chair.
Living outside for forty-three days,

scrambling slopes and ringing
a dinner bell — the pitch makes you mental.
There's no time except mealtime,
no correspondence between words:
red rot, bagging out, slash and cache whores.

One morning your site's blotted with clumps
of brown fur, reeks like turned earth and saliva.
Before you swallow the cold or realize
maturity isn't something you can work on,
you crawl on all fours, gather up
remains to forge another animal.

Buried Animals

I conflated pecking order with
fulfillment. What I've given
is no longer where you left it.

I am the spectrum of uncertainty
in the grand scheme of lost things.
You are the irreversible find:
a chipped clamshell of over-share.

You can barely contain yourself.
Glisten. Each comment reaches
a depth determined by your siphons.
Buried treasure to be mapped, later.

I watch the tidal flats for bubbles.
You don't know what you're doing
but you're sure you're looking.

I can't think of what else
to say to you about molluscs.
They're common and rarely alone.

Ringling

The argument
one-upped your one-man show,
left hand wrestling
the right, declaring
I'd be sorry one day.
Swallowing chicken heads whole
you've weaned yourself of taste
at the centre of the sideshow.
I never took a turn.
My job was to relieve
customers of the ghosts
that spoiled a pristine aura.
My X-ray vision
illuminated dead relatives,
lurking behind the living.
They'd trust me, just thrilled
to be noticed. I'd lure
spirits close then carve
them out of this world
with an ivory pocket knife.
I kept their glowing orbs
in Mason jars,
which sold for four dollars.
The argument was about
whether this was fair.
I'm sorry I had to see
your coat of tar and chicken feathers.
People paid for this privilege.
I shot myself out of a cannon
to lighten the mood,
grew a beard and the dog
wouldn't stop barking
at me. Your need to distinguish

yourself from all the men
who tattooed my name
into their flesh ruined us.
The argument was
our interpretative walk.
It started when you started it.

To a Point

You'd chase me to my flights then, waving
from the bottom of the escalator at my back.
I'd wonder where to rest my insomnia, how
to go round-trip without returning to you.

A contract on the table is just a smaller,
white table, made to be put upon.

I haven't moved in ages. In dreams,
I still don't. There are no messages.
What happened to the perfect voyage
scene we chipped away?

With the time travel of jet lag between us,
it's late enough to call forth drink or purge
all the boxes packed with half-lives.

Any sense of myself will resume
when I wake to the fact of altitude.

I haven't stayed overnight in ages,
sleep's easy to like and hard to know.

Homecoming

You're at the Kal Tire in Vanderhoof
when the first signs of life climb out
the back of a Suburban, tossing a cape
of muck across your dungarees. I wait

until you leave town to flog my sorry.
You're stranded at the camp scales.
I predict an abandoned food processor
discovered in your brain's pleasure centre,

that you'll barbel your way to the crick.
I still itch for your closet room — so cold,
spectral breaths spooked our sleep, for
dry humping till someone's zipper breaks.

It will sting, taste bitter, when you hear
what I've done. Your face crests, bushward.

Driving 25 Sideroad, North of 30

I've nailed down where
I fell in love with the world
to a particular stretch of drive.

Four towns flung along
my chosen route. I bet on
which place's future is fated
to creepy pit stops, arid gas pipes.
It costs to pluck them out.

Windshield glare morphs
a row crop into a tornado,
which rips barn walls
into picture windows.

Scent of cut hay stirs an old bruise
to ache: a mark worth questioning.
So much seems inevitable.

Young: on the riding mower
in open-toed jelly shoes.

Fledgling: the site of lust's first spark,
I was directionless, on fire.

Now: my car, open windows;
the a/c vent gifts me a cough's worth
of dust, and still moves me.

Finding oneself is a chore.
I want the wild impulses
of another's troubles.

We're at that age

when our childhood pets are dying.

Age seven, summer, walking shoeless
on the gravel roads to toughen up my feet.
By August I'd be calloused, floating
above the coals of ground like a saint.

Those roads are paved now. You can pass the farms
faster. On this stretch, my father used to jolt me
out of backseat boredom, shouting *Deer!*
but every time I looked, the same slow cows.

I am controlled by this promise. To see
a thing less fragile but just as strange
and worthy. Like a seagull is an eagle
to each memory, perfect in its place.

Acknowledgements

In the poem "Fraterville Coal Mine," the italicized lines are from a letter written by Jacob Vowell to his wife, Ellen, while he was trapped and suffocating in the Fraterville, Tennessee, coal mine disaster of 1902. Source: United Mine Workers of America. See "Oh God for one more breath," *Letters of Note* (blog), January 23, 2014, http://www.lettersofnote. com/2014/01/oh-god-for-one-more-breath.html.

Earlier versions of some of these poems have appeared in the *Fiddlehead*, *PANK Magazine*, the *Malahat Review*, the *Puritan*, *Riddle Fence*, *Minola Review*, *This Magazine*, *PRISM international*, and in the chapbook *Playdate* by Anstruther Press. My thanks to the editors of these publications.

I am grateful to the Canada Council for the Arts, the Social Sciences and Humanities Research Council, and the Toronto Arts Council for financial assistance that allowed me to write this book.

Many thanks to the Banff Centre for the Arts and the University of Guelph for their generous support.

Gratitude: Al Moritz. Ross Leckie. John Barton. Catherine Bush. John Shoptaw. Bob Pickering. Dionne Brand. Everyone at Goose Lane.

Thanks to brilliant advice-giver and confidant Kevin Connolly. Thanks to mentor of mentors Karen Solie. Extra thanks to an incisive and wonderful editor, Linda Besner.

XO:

Damir, for encouraging me in the first place. Friends who have humoured my first drafts, sat through readings, and bolstered me with their love. AA, KB, LB, LJ, RG, AGR, AI, AK, HL, AP, RR, OS, CT, DW. Dear pups of Waldorf, Peterborough, Dartmouth, Fredericton, and Toronto. Jim Johnstone. Michael Prior. The LDC. UNB-ers. Guelph MFA classmates. Banff soulmates, especially Wes. Soul sister — Nadine. Cousin Jackie. Lifers — Maya and Sarah. True blue — Doyle. Makers — the very best mum and bro; my dad, Tony, who was unfalteringly supportive.

photo: Nadine Sander-Green

Allison LaSorda grew up in Campbellville, Ontario, and after some years in the Maritimes now lives in Toronto. A recipient of scholarships from the Banff Centre Writing Studio and the Vermont Studio Center, she holds an MFA from the University of Guelph. Her writing has appeared in *PANK Magazine*, *PRISM international*, *Brick*, *Riddle Fence*, the *Malahat Review*, the *Fiddlehead*, and others.